Time Frame

Other books by Bonnie Beatson Palmquist:

Voices of Minnesota History: 1836-1946 (Galde Press, 2000)

Time Frame

Bonnie Beatson Palmquist

2003
Galde Press, Inc.
Lakeville, Minnesota, U.S.A.

Time Frame
© Copyright 2003 by Bonnie Beatson Palmquist
All rights reserved.
Printed in the United States of America
No part of this book may be used or reproduced in any manner whatsoever without written permission from the publishers except in the case of brief quotations embodied in critical articles and reviews.

First Edition
First Printing, 2003

Cover photograph reproduced with permission of Minnesota Historical Society

Galde Press, Inc.
PO Box 460
Lakeville, Minnesota 55044–0460

For John, Anne, Steve, and Mary,
Greg, Rich, Jamie, and Bill

Contents

Acknowledgements — xv

I. Time Frame

Time Frame — 3

Face — 7

Endless Days — 9

The Ghost Garden — 11

An Eagle's Flight — 13

Apart So Long — 15

Portrait of 48 Hours — 19

Second Encounter — 21

Vulnerable Time — 23

Waiting at the Top of the Stairs for My Granddaughter to Finish Her Climb — 25

Tuesday Night, Wednesday Morning — 27

1121 Revisited — 29

Lament for My Family Name — 31

Title/Name — 33

Red Wing ... 35

Crow ... 37

Lemon ... 39

Bad Scene ... 41

Night Nurse ... 43

Not Random ... 45

Give Me Your Hand: Challenger Elegy ... 47

II. One With All

Partial Vision ... 51

Not Long Enough ... 53

Sister ... 55

Space and Time ... 57

The Day the Calendar Stopped ... 59

The Fourth Spring ... 61

Picture ... 63

III. Looking Down the Road

August 1934	67
A Summer Day: Underwood, 1910	69
January/1975	71
The Ice House	73
Canoe Country	75
Summer Times Three	77
White Light	79
The Cricket Month	81
Ballooning	83
Dog Walkers	85
Q&A	89
Window Washers	91
"Snow Scene"	93
Sudden Stop	95
The Barn	97

IV. Tender the Words

Windsong	101
23 E. Front Street: Self-Portrait in Second Person	103
Summit Avenue	105
Summer Song	107
Regions of the Moon	109
On Reading William Stafford's "Traveling Through the Dark"	111
Pencil Drawings	113
When I Die	115
The Whole Truth, You Say	117
The Time	119
Alto	121
Duet With Paul Zweig	123
The Reunion, The Photograph, The Few	125
Final Notice	127
The Used Book Sale	129
"All My Love"	131
May You Fare Well	133

Elegy	135
Before Dawn	137
November Gray	139
A Litany of Thanksgiving for the Sense of God in my World	141
Dreamfields	143

Acknowledgements

"A Summer Day: Underwood, 1910"
    Sites and Sights Traveling Exhibit,
    The History Museum of East Otter Tail County (Minn.), 2001
"Night Nurse," *Sidewalks,* Fall/Winter 2000-2001.
"On Reading William Stafford's 'Traveling Through the
    Dark,'" *Loonfeather,* Fall/Winter 1988.
"Redwing," *Dust and Fire 2002,* Bemidji University.
"Summer Song," *Loonfeather,* Fall/Winter 1988.
"Title/Name," *Re-Imagining,* November 2001

I am grateful to my friend and mentor, Deborah Keenan, and the members of my writing group for their help and support.

I. Time Frame

Time Frame
for my children

I.

I never thought about it that way,
the names, events and places
I grew up with have no meaning for you.
So familiar to me, the milestones
and reference points of my life,
ancient history to you.
Perhaps no history at all.

As people disappear, buildings vanish,
events fade, I see part of what I was
disappear with them.
Now, I struggle to find new names,
places, and events to relate to you.
I never thought about it that way,
how my time frame evolves, dissolves
becomes another.

II.

*I never thought about it this way
the names, events, and places
that mean so much to you
I barely know or barely remember.
That you might find it hard
to know my world. The present world.
I only look forward.
My world holds promise.*

*Buildings built on recycled lands
are my points of reference.
Names familiar to me
are unknown to you. The world whirls
faster than I can keep up.*

III.

I tell you of my history,
part of your history.
The time frame between yours and mine—
this space we share right now.

Face

The old mirror with its ornate brackets
        hung in the upstairs hall,
                silent observer of the household.

Faces looked into its depths and hoped
        to see: a younger face, a prettier face, an older face.

I longed to grow taller and enter the world.

But the small face remained the same,
        eyes reaching for the future,
                before the bride's image appeared.

I left the house, the mirror;
        my face began to change.
                The mirror came to me.

As the face grows older,
    the hidden image of who I am
        is found in silver splinters,
            sheltered within its frame,
                mute and undefeated.

Endless Days

The sudden wind of warmth
engulfs me in memory,

takes me to time where games played
lengthened afternoon into evening,
when street lights arched
like fingers in the sky,
flashing their diamond rings.

The dusk echoed with calls of
"ole, ole, olson freedom,"
until the deep night
brought sleep undisturbed.

The streets are quiet now,
the games forgotten.
The dusk is peopled with phantom voices
travelling through time, calling me in,
calling me home.

The Ghost Garden

Somewhere in the ghost garden
of white flowers are memories
of my grandmother's garden
filled with old fashioned flowers.
Bridal wreath fell gracefully.
White french lilacs fronted her mugo pine
background for purple irises,
swordlike in their beauty.

Four o'clocks announced the afternoon.
Hollyhocks for her grandchildren to make dolls.
When night fell, faint light
was caught in white begonias
ringing the apple tree. I think of her often
although I can no longer hear her voice.
Yet, I can see her working in the garden,
smiling as I came to call, a small child
who now has a ghost garden shining
with memories as gentle as her spirit.

An Eagle's Flight

My brother was an eagle,
circling the world,
held aloft by thermal
winds of war and peace.
Vanishing for years,
then alighting briefly
on the bare branch of home.
Eager to be with him,
I could not join him.
Always out of reach,
always majestic,
always an idol.

My brother was an eagle
with a broken wing,
forced to descend
to the ground. I found
a man I did not know.
Late, we began again.

My brother was
finally brought to rest
with a caisson as a cage.
an eagle on his shoulder.
Entombed with comrades.
lighted by eternal flame.

I go to see him
perched on a hill,
with all the ranks
who chorus of great
and glorious deeds
I never knew.

My brother in his absence
felt familiar, the
space he filled
stayed filled, now with
grief and questions.

Apart So Long

We leave and arrive in many ways.
He stayed behind, starting his life without them
as they left for a new house and city.
He began to experience the freedom
he had always wanted—
no longer a member of his father's house,
under his father's rule. Able now
to declare his objection to the war,
even as his father supported it.

A rocky start to adulthood.
He found being on one's own
was not what he had anticipated.
Found he hadn't been prepared
for the empty void he felt
as the airplane departed.

He struggled to find work, finish school,
find his way. He seldom returned,
four years passed, one time
without connection.
Poverty sometimes kept us
from him, and he from us.
Apart so long he didn't recognize
his brother at the airport.
A long time before
finally making his peace
with his father, with his family.

On his 40th birthday,
his brothers and sisters surprised him,
claimed him as their own
ending a long journey of estrangement.
His was the first of many leavings,
others left as their worlds
expanded, but without the anger.

We leave and arrive in many ways,
grateful when the return journey
becomes easier. Reclaimed,
he is a part of his family,
scattered far from each other,
but no farther away than
a phone call in time of need.
Bonds strong enough to close the circle,
to arrive at the beginning.

Portrait of 48 Hours

All we had was the day between,
a full day to compress years apart.
A weekend you said, I can come.

The day you came, a flight delayed
took hours away from us. The day to leave,
an early flight took you home.

All we had was the day between.

The day was full, talk abundant,
an artificial atmosphere
to make every moment count.
Cram memories to take home.

Time distilled leaving only the day between
to mend the fences, to recall the bonds
that made us family, made us friends.

Second Encounter

You walk back into my life,
older now, wiser now,
ignoring the wasted years
that lay between us

in a relationship that had
nowhere to go.
You stir up the waters
finally calmed to glass.

Muddy the past
with your ill-remembered events.
What do you want of me?
I cannot reorder the past,

I can't give you what you want:
a chance to live your life over.

Vulnerable Time

To share our love
for the rest of our lives,
gives me the courage
to face my average life.

In the darkness,
lying in your arms,
I am content and at peace.

You understand
the gentle touch,
the affectionate smile,
cements the bonds between us.

The night
holds no fear for me.

We will go on together
toward the unknown,
confident the darkness
will end in light.

I know I will go on,
will survive without you,
but having had your love,
I know what I have lost.

In the darkness
alone with only my dream,
you return and I feel your touch.

It's the touch I miss most,
a gentle caress on my cheek,
a quick hug when we parted,
a warm embrace after a journey.

My loneliness
comes in the night.

If I can know
we will be together again,
then I can better confront
the darkness.

Waiting at the Top of the Stairs for My Granddaughter to Finish Her Climb

It could have been the scent of peonies,
those harbingers of a Northern spring
that race for the sky overnight,
and instantly transport me

back to childhood, back to
treasured early morning walks,
the quiet neighborhood
where I sat on the top of steep steps
that led to St. Clair avenue. The city before me
like a miniature board game. I dreamed:
great adventures, long journeys.

A humble place to have such power
to invoke such longing for that time and place.
Even now when I pass these steep stairs,
I want to stop.

Tuesday Night

I am waiting for my visitors.
To hear what has happened
in their lives. I've shared their sorrows,
joys, marriages, births. In comparison my life

has been uneventful, ordinary.

I'll hear of the latest problems,
complications in this fictional family
I know better than my own family.

How did that happen?

Wednesday Morning

I relate to this family that doesn't exist
Whose lives are determined by a writer
putting words in their mouths.
Whose actions have no consequences.

All families have problems, consequences

that can't be solved in an hour.
Do I take refuge from circumstances
I have no control over? Or am I lonely?

How it happened.

1121 Revisited

My childhood home is being moved
to satisfy the expansive needs
of a school I did not attend.

My anchor in the town
I grew up in. A thread to peonies
and lilacs of my youth, broken.

Soon an anchor for your family,
plant peonies, plant lilacs,
harvest your dreams, your memories.

Lament for My Family Name

I go sometimes to see my name,
now found only in graveyards
half buried under fallen leaves,
like severed limbs of the family tree.
Proudly worn in my childhood
now this branch is barren.

I carry another name
borrowed by convention
but that is not who I am.

My name comes
from the lowlands of Scotland.
My name sailed on canvas wings,
two small children cradled
in strong, hopeful arms.

My family far from its origins
had many sons now dead
who took the name with them.
Daughters were left nameless.

Now the name is done.

Title/Name

When you go thru life with one name,
then change it how does it affect you?

When the titles you bear change
are you the sum of them or do you

start again with a new identity?

Names, random letters
attached to things and people.

To fill the spaces we call reality.
we add titles and names.

Red Wing

Small particles of the day,
reluctant to end the glow

are caught in the milky whiteness
of Queen Anne's Lace
floating in the cup of night.

Blue black rolling hills
wrapped in charcoal.

Our shadows blend, a small sigh
close by;

we wait as the night
takes the day,

part of the wind slipping
past the hours.

Crow

High on a slender thread
of bough twisting through
a black skeleton of summer,
my raucous cry
calls the meeting to order.
I am magnificent, my inky
black feathers
spread wide
upon the evening sky.
I perch on
the tallest branch,
arrange myself
in courtly manner.
My fellow scavengers
wheel and hang glide
survey their domain.
Wide wings and curved claws

settle into arched portals
as the flock
joins in a clamorous bid
to be heard.

The meetings continue
until my purple cloak,
shimmering in bright sunlight
escapes my house confines,
spreads over jet black feathers
and I fly with them.
Dwellings recede
as currents lift
my outstretched glossy
wings. Free.
I soar with them,
seeing all I wish
I had known
before the raucous cries
came for me.

Lemon

Tart, like the unsweetened word
of rejection, its taste acquired.
Sunny among oranges, apples,
plums from trees given to excess.

Its tangy flavor
a counterpoint to the juicy,
crunchy taste of its cousins.
Its mission: to enhance the ordinary.

Cool lemon, refreshes a hot day,
is essential for barbecue, loves fish
passionately. Its zest to enrich,
like a friend who inspires you.

Bad Scene

slick road, icy surface
twisted car, jagged parts
crumpled hood, fenders
lights flash red
plenty of blood.

the wreckage, the glass
the bones, the lives
bad luck, bad karma,
bad dream, bad scene.

Night Nurse

Crepe soled shoes
step into the night
shadows, dim lights,
hushed corridors.

A ring away from
the fretful sleep
patterns the sick
try to escape.

The night hours,
slow as a heartbeat
near collapse. Only
the monitor ticks.

Not Random

If you would ask me why
a few random notes of music
could move me to tears
I could not tell you.
Of all the combinations
of sounds, those send me
to a time, a place
where emotions buried deep
would open a tenderness
without a name.
Poignant, fleeting,
moments of love, sorrow,
and hope. Age has made
the past present.
A response intimate, personal,
a yearning for time to reverse itself,
hear for the first time,
know the melody that follows.

Give Me Your Hand: Challenger Elegy

We know the end, now,
hurtling through the ether of space.
We knew the risks we faced,
but with smile and wave,
not looking at the blue sky as a killer,
we entered a world we knew.
Tightly strapped into cushions
that would serve us as our coffins,
we departed.
And only seconds later
our deaths came toward us,
and one of us said, "Give me your hand,"
and one of us began to answer.

II. One With All

Partial Vision

Who were you?
We were never close.
You, a woman raised in that time,
never said, "I love you,"
(but you did.)
How was I to know
you were proud of me?
You never told me.
You died so long ago
I cannot hear your voice.

"What delightful daughters you have,"
they said.
Look who their mother is,"
you replied.
I thought that so vain of you.
Now I know you only wanted recognition.

You were a woman trapped
in the circumstances of your life—
what could you have done
had you lived in my time?

It took courage in 1912 to marry
outside your religion and nationality.
Courage to travel, after marriage,
to small towns to collect money
for your law book firm.

I inherited my love of books,
my sayings from you.
In the hospital at the end,
I had to leave you, unconscious,
never having a chance to say,
"I love you."
No, I had the chance, but I was
held back by constraints
of childhood, powerful as the love
I meant to speak.

Not Long Enough

A surprised older father
on the edges of my life.
Not the father
of my older brother and sisters.

You said, "I wouldn't take a million
dollars for one of my children,
but I wouldn't give a nickel for another one."

I remember Sundays—
you had breakfast waiting
when we came home from church.
You took me to Indian Mounds Park
to gaze at the skyline of St. Paul.

A born salesman, but gone too often,
you took me on a trip to Eau Claire,
I don't remember what we talked about,
maybe we didn't talk.

You died the month before
I graduated from high school.
When I made my entrance,
I looked up beyond the balcony,
hoping you knew how I missed you/how I wished/
I had known you better.

Sister

There was a time we shared,
when I was young, you the older sister.
We walked to Mass
through the stillness
of early morning Lent
to the brick walled convent,
to quiet sounds
of women's voices,
caroled Gregorian chants.
behind carved wooden screens.

Flickering candles,
smell of incense.

A closeness between us
which would not come again.

You left my world.

Later, we returned
to the city of our birth.
Family bonds claimed us for a moment.

You greeted me with adult voice.
Always ready to listen to me,
you kept your thoughts
locked up.

I watched you grow thin,
your voice grow silent
as the cancer advanced.
I could only tell you
I loved you and would miss you,
though I did not know
what those words meant
to you, to me.

Space and Time
for my sister, Jean, thirteen years after—

How many times do we lose someone?
Once as they are dying, again at the funeral.
Then begins a long time of little losses.

When I walk into her home, I can still
see her smile of welcome, her graciousness
reflected in her home as she left it.

The house now slated for dismantling,
the essence of her, lost piece by piece
as the things she loved and cherished

are dispersed into strangers' hands.
When that is done there is no longer
a space filled with her presence.

Only in my mind's eye will she open
the door, reach out, draw me into
this inner space—memory.

The Day the Calendar Stopped

The hospital draws us night and day.
Odd, she has seen more
of her family, (sometimes
recognizing them, sometimes
not), than she had in months.

At the end, my sister's
mouth gasps for air,
her eyes partially open,
panicked to breathe,
her labored breath
comes slower and slower.

I see the skeleton
face of my mother and sister.

I hold her hand, tell
her to let go,
to go home, find peace.
She does.

My reluctant eyes gaze
into the coffin and find my sister,
younger and beautiful.
The pain gone
erasing the distorted image
of the day the calendar stopped.

The Fourth Spring

Each spring for three years
some one in my family has died,
oldest to the youngest.

The first spring, my brother, far from me
in time and space left without a farewell.

The next spring, my older sister, who trusted
her doctor and should not have, died.

Last spring my other sister died,
slowly. That leaves me.

I've kept myself from winter's cold,
wrapped myself in hope for life.

And now it's spring again,
I surround myself
with riot of flowers,
hear a peaceful, secret waterfall.

My house is in order;
I walk into the world,
not waiting.

Picture

Why did they have
a hand colored picture
of a lone palm tree
rising alone on a deserted beach
with dune color sand
white capped waves
disappearing into indigo water?

Who bought it? He or She?

Long after the picture
was packed away
it remains an enigma.
How little is revealed
of its owners,
who bought an artificial world
that never existed.

Two people
saw a lone palm tree
in a fantasy world
and waited, waited
for the tree to sway.

III. Looking Down the Road

August 1934

Her small body curled
    to fit into the ledge
        behind the car's back seat.

Looking out the oval window
    the sky retreated,

The telephone poles marched
    in quick step to disappear
        like a thread of wire.

A never ending view,
    like a movie going backwards.
        she rode into memory.

A Summer Day: Underwood, 1910

Fishing rods in their hands,
    my mother and her sisters stand
        proudly with their catch of fish.

Smiling, posing for the camera,
    flowered hats, shirtwaists,
        long flowing skirts.

Their bonnets so alluring,
    did the fish leap to see?

Close to shore, weeds bend
    in a slight breeze. The lakeshore
        a dark line on the horizon.

A day to feel warm sun, companionship.
    Did the boat rock when they carefully
        sat down? Who did the rowing?

January/1975

I start out in the warm, mild January Day
that turns into a nightmare.

Rain becomes snow, slants sideways.
The roadbed a sheet of ice.
Cars unable to stay on the road,
slide crossways before landing

in the ditch.
Unable to turn back, I continue,
hands frozen to the wheel.
The wind blows sweeping mounds.

A whiteout. No longer able to see
road or a welcoming driveway,

I knew how immigrants felt,
lost on the prairie,
far from the lights that awaited them,

stumbling, searching for the rope
that would lead them home.

I search for the road,
hidden as deeply as the lost rope
their hands searched for
in the white.

The Ice House

Sometimes when I hear the ice crackling
underneath my feet, I think of the night

we were stranded far from shore.
The ice house no longer a refuge,

cracks widening before us. Too late,
warning signs ignored, like our trust

in each other. When did the ice become porous,
threaded with bubbles of air

waiting for the first false step?

Canoe Country

Color changes subtly from blue to silver to white,
the light from day washed air blankets the ground
of snow like a carelessly thrown quilt,
mounding over rocks and fallen trees.
A path trampled by footsteps leads to the lake,
now shielded in formless ice, windswept by arctic winds that
play between stands of pine trees huddled against the shore.
A wisp of smoke drifts upward, disappears

like the voyagers of the north. Small, sturdy French Canadians,
who paddled birchbark canoes through rivers and lakes,
crossed portages filled with biting black flies, carried cargos
of furs for the rich in Europe who wore high crowned hats.

The house tucked into the hillside catches the last faint light
of day. The time when one can almost hear the voyagers' chant.

Summer Times Three

June

Anticipate soft winds,
flowers with halos of color,
the lushness of time.
Spell of June
waits for the unknown
visitor to arrive.

July

White sun, blue sky,
motionless shade,
riotous flowers.
July's breath as fiery
as our encounter
in a sun drenched
world of possibilities.

August

Long, lazy month
of heated nights,
darkness lit by fireflies
winking above the garden's
tired remnants,
ends the lushness of June,
ends the sweet summertime
love shared with you.

White Light

After "Primavera Amarilla"
Juan Ramon Jimenez

My pale white hands, God, were never
meant to hold the dead, their skeleton
white bones devoid of life. Instead
I ask blessings today upon trees,
garlands of vines.

Pristine white roses
and pale butterflies line silver waters
holding blue white lilies filled with moon light
in a world of filtered sun.

Love blossoms
like the flowering white apple orchard.
The cemetery, down the hill
meets one white washed fence,
guards a silver brook and snow white flowers
belonging to the month of white light, July.

The Cricket Month

In August, the rhythmic sounds in the darkness
tell of heat and time; the month of the crickets.

In the stillness of a lazy afternoon
and the gathering darkness of evening,

the sound signals the return of autumn,
when the wind and rain come from a different direction.

They are joined by the droning, high pitched sound
of the cicadas, a counterpoint for the steady beat.

The earth cools and the days grow longer
without the friendliness of a small chirping sound.

Nature's clock ticking away with small beats,
ticking away until all is quiet.
And the winter winds arrive.

Ballooning

I float above trees   in the silence of the air
    lazily seek the horizon   a line from then to now

drift on a soft wind   unable to catch the shadow
    glide over indigo water   filled with white butterflies of sails

soar over a patchwork quilt of farm fields   waiting for the harvest
    descend into gullies   rise into tree tops

a crayon box of colors balloon above us   warm air lifts us to the clouds
    a river stream loops like a shiny necklace

I hear delighted laughter   see sun filled vistas   feel airy freedom
    gently we descend   glide to the earth   end a peaceful journey
        with eyes of renewed clarity

Dog Walkers

Never underestimate
the importance of
professional dog walkers,
guiding man's best friends
along the walk of life.
Allowing them to sniff
each lamppost and curb
to see what friends
had left calling cards.

Their charges prance
as if they know
they are the elite
of the canine world.
Prestige, too belongs
to dog walkers of rare
and expensive breeds
Allows hauteur in their walk,
enhances their status.

In New York, you
see them with five dogs
pulling on leashes
eager to investigate
the concrete canyons.
Never dreaming
of roaming
the green fields
of their country cousins.
Never the freedom
to race and meet
their owners
home from school.

Content to have
what is offered:
a leash, an elevator,
a dog walker.

Q&A

Why say
the moon
is blue?
You color
with
your mood.

Why ask
what can't
be answered?
The question
has not
been asked.

Why skate
on thin ice?
When water
disappears
you are grounded.

Window Washers

view the world, straight on,
sometimes reflected
in sheets of molten light.

Climbing glassy heights
secure in harnesses that float
in a sea of air; ready to rid the world

of grime; ready to swing
tethered only by wings of steel.

"Snow Scene"

was the title the artist gave it. I call it,
"Four O'Clock on a January Afternoon."
A lake, a cabin, trees, and solitude.

Winter's thin light fades into
the lake's blue whiteness.
Pine trees laden with snow.
Smoke drifts from the chimney
of the cabin tucked into the hill.
It is the quiet time of the day.

In summer's heat, I pause in front of it,
become immersed in the stillness,
the whiteness, the quiet peace it reflects.
The purity of the scene compels.
the quiet peace it reflects.

In dim twilight the scene
gains an added depth,
snow deeper on the trees,
cabin more secluded,
coldness more penetrating.

It hangs over the fireplace,
over the fires of October
that draw eyes inward,
to become mesmerized, to dream,
before the time of deep winter.

Sudden Stop

The other stranger watches
rescue attempts
to revive the man.
Flashing bulbs spun
a broken wave of light.
Two strangers alive,
two cars behind.

The Barn

Go
through tall doors
    of weathered pine cut from century old
    stands of white pine, hewed by
        hands calloused and rough; working hands. Walk

on
floors grooved with
    years of cows going out to pasture.
    Their tails flicking flies, their
        heads in sweet grass. Waiting for the bell

to
call them home.
    Season after season this faint trail
    of ground gives mute witness
        to clopping sounds of returning cows

Smell
the air filled
  with ancient grain dust. Sunlight filters
  through cracks, shadows criss cross
    stalls, empty as the farmstead dwelling.

Now
abandoned,
  the stone foundation firm as the faith
  of people who built it.
    Its walls collapsed from storms yield to

the
suburb's growth.
  See the land tilled into one acre plots,
  planted with houses, roads
    overlaying a farmer's vision.

IV. Tender the Words

Windsong

Invade
my soul
music
sing for
me. Those
who do
not hear
with hearts,
songs go
unheard
fleeting
wind   gone.

23 E. Front Street: Self-Portrait in Second Person

She stood in the doorway, sheltered, waiting.
The street was rainswept and empty.
Sounds muffled and distant.
The houses wrapped in silence.
Window shades tightly drawn
keep those inside secluded
from their neighbors' lives
Blank eyes always turning inward.
She wanted to flee
from these deserted streets,
the world they rejected.

Rain changed to mist
softening harsh angles.
Her body stood alert, waiting.
She saw the approaching car,
its head lights two arrows
knifing through the mist.
This was her escape to—where?
she didn't know.
She stepped from the doorway,
the shades of her home wide open,
her movement
a choice.

Summit Avenue

The same streets, yet not,
generations add
imprints with a fluid light.

I see with my parents' eyes,
I walk in my parents' steps,

down sidewalks filled
with images, what I see
transcends the decades.

My parents' time faded,
My time fades
to my children's.

But the same solid
structures define
this place, this city.

An avenue to my past,
of generations
reaching from
one century to another.

My children see. And in their time
their children will see
images that transcend the decades.
Images established, so
grounded in place,

they carry our history forward,
no sign of effort in the fluid light.

Summer Song

I sit on the porch to read
listen to the summer sounds.
Muted voices carol through the dusk;
crickets mark endless time.
A barking dog fences with an unknown shadow.
Soft sounds of sleepy birds,
faint music of wind chimes
stir a longing unnamed.
A sprinkler's hypnotic rhythm.
A horn's blare, shattering the stillness.
I sit on the porch, read
and wonder if these summer sounds
are heard by you, my unknown friend.

Regions of the Moon

Lost from the regions of the moon,
the river shrouded in gray mist
covers the land with ledges of vapor
shields life with silver edges.

The disoriented landscape veils
a foreign land, a domain without life.

The mist lightens, creates a vista bathed
in somber shades, formless shadows.
The water warms the breeze.

The shroud lifts, life takes over from veil,
from mist, and earth reclaims its edges.

On Reading William Stafford's "Traveling Through the Dark"

I would have saved the fawn,
innocent, waiting to be born.
mute inside the dark cavity.
Slowly the heartbeat stills,
darkness deepens,
life ends swiftly
in black water
chilling the warmth
of a mother's womb.
I would have saved the fawn.

Pencil Drawings

I use shadows of gifts,
for if only the most musical
birds were allowed to sing
woods would be a more quiet place.

Words like pencil drawings,
are shaded with fine detail,
ask you to look
beyond the delicate strokes
to see with the writer's eye.
Frames the image with minute detail.
Shades the whole as lines become subtle
determined by the eye of the reader.

In shadows I tender the words,
the paper, hesitant to reveal,
yet choose to hum a few hushed notes
into the quiet woods.

When I Die

When I die
someone hold my hand,
and pass it on
to the outstretched
hands waiting for me.

Nurturing hands
that held me gently,
fed and clothed me.
Hands that reached back
to help me find my way.

Hands I never knew:
tiny hands
of my miscarried child,
careworn hands
of the grandmother
who named me.

All those who were,
so I am.

When my turn comes
to take my place,
I'll wait for you
and take your hand
and pass it on
to the unseen Hand
that holds us all.

The Whole Truth, You Say

If I chose
to believe
only part of it, will I
understand that
which I believe?
I am caught
between two
viewpoints. I am
not wise enough
to know what is
withheld.   Truth
lies somewhere
in the middle.

The Time

"This is what you wanted"
Kathleen Anderson

This is what
you wanted.

Your life to
have meaning.

To continue
the stories
that are your
legacy.

To be a
bridge
for future
generations.

A feeling
of peace
knowing you
have done all
you could do
to hold those
you love
together,

for the time
you have left.

Alto

for Pat

You cannot
ascend
into the heavens,
carry the melody
skyward.

Your voice
is grounded
to the earth;
to anchor.

Voices
intertwine
become one
like a woven cloth
of light and dark
strands.

Each voice
weaves a strand
of color,
depth of emotion that covers all
who hear, who sing.

You are
the delicate balance
that makes melodies whole.

Your voice
underscores
the timbre, emotion,
the joy
of creation.

You are
in the shadows
helping make the glory
of this fine tapestry.

Duet With Paul Zweig

Roads trickling uphill like weak desires
lead downward to the valley
where they configured into one.
The one I had looked for and lost.
Now the beginning was at the end,
desires a strong reason to live.

With a single car moving along main street,
(parade of one), the town came to a halt
and watched as I searched for the house
described in the letter, the house of grandparents
I never met. Now mine with all its secrets
still intact. It's an old town with houses clustered
near sidewalks of octagon stones.
Their windows stare at me.

Like exhausted blood returning to the heart
this house, its wide lawns, ancient spreading trees
offered the refuge I so sorely needed.
Lives here were lived quietly yet were part
of town life. **Always different, always the same.**
Now another generation gains what others had.
My grandparents known in name only; their daughter, my mother.
Through her this house was waiting for me.

Which makes memory an entirely mysterious act
a collective knowledge gathered in many generations
now mine to assimilate. **Like the sound barrier expanding
behind the plane,** my experiences made an added dimension
to life within this dwelling. **Without any coming or going**
I found my place, **with an idea of stillness, extent without duration.**

The Reunion, The Photograph, The Few

Who are these people
come to renew friendships
created in their youth?
Eager to see someone
whose last contact was long ago.
Grateful the name tags are in big letters,
grateful they are able to walk, to hear.
Many are missing from this 50th reunion;
dead; not able to come;
disenchanted with the whole idea.

Bright smiles for the camera belying
white hair, no hair, canes and hearing aids.
Painful reminders of fifty years
after youthful hopes and dreams.
So few I remember, I recognize
Young faces disappeared, morphing
into experienced lines of living.

The photograph will be compared to the last one
noting more empty spaces.
Who will be missing next reunion.
When will I disappear into empty space?

Final Notice

i. The obituary section of the paper is often
the last as if the end of the paper was the end.

Name, age, place of death, survivors.
If they lived long enough,
or were rich and famous enough,
almost a whole story might emerge.

For most people the notice was modest,
brevity masking the grief of the family.

ii The saddest of all were the children
who struggled to overcome illness.
Babies, stillborn, or who only lived a few hours or days.
The parents writing this notice
instead of a joyous one.

iii. Today's notices are not like the obituaries
of former times. Those often contained
flowery descriptions of the person's life.
"A woman of meritorious qualities,"
or "a man as an upstanding member
of the community."

iv. Epidemics filled the paper with names of victims,
often the youngest and most vulnerable.

v. If you wrote your obituary what would you write
after the normal facts are recited?
What do you hope the response would be?

That your legacy holds honor.
That you will be missed.

The Used Book Sale

From the piles of books waiting for new owners,
the blue one fell open to the title page.
An inscription dedicated to:

"My friend, Robert,
you have made such a difference in my life
and will continue to do so. Best Wishes, John Tower"

How was his life changed? Why did one's actions affect
others in such a profound way?

"Happy 10th Birthday, Tommy."

Tommy, now a grown man
does he remember who gave him this?

> *"Looking forward to our*
> *'Cup of Christmas Tea' Love, Aunt Ellen."*

Aunt Ellen, now dead, is there still another
"Cup of Christmas Tea" served?

> *"All my love, all my life, Bill"*

Why was this book given to the sale
carrying such a poignant inscription?

Scribbled inscriptions, faded, forgotten
are inspirations for my next book:
"All My Love"

"All My Love"

I sat looking at this small volume,
pages creased, well used.
Poems of Robert Browning
"How do I love thee"
familiar to all of us, but having
special meaning for two people.

Where was he now? Dead or disappeared
like the love he professed.
Someone had treasured this book
and its giver. Was she gone
and her house dismantled?

I like to think this couple
shared the reading, loved the words,
rather than the love grew cold
and distant. I thought of books
I had inscribed to my love
in our early courtship.
I mean every word—then.

May You Fare Well

Dear friend leaving so suddenly and unexpectedly.
May you find peace in the coming place you will live.
May you find friends as devoted to you as you have here.
May you know your place in my life will never be filled
by anyone so understanding, so compassionate, and supportive.
May your heart be lightened, your spirit renewed.
May you fare well in the coming years.

Elegy

> *"I will stand, a tree, here,*
> *never to know another spot."*
> May Swenson

Grounded forever among my family,
    long gone and newly arrived,

the fourth generation nestles near
    the woman who haunts me, her tiny babies,

men who left the blighted crops of Ireland
    and planted themselves in this soil.

Crowded with names of Barry and McMahon,
    my sister and I the last

to encircle the roots grown deeply
        enough to anchor my family here.

Ancient trees, firmly rooted, hold fast.
    I slowly become
        one with all.

Before Dawn

The night darkness
      brings somber thoughts
      no logic—no faith,
      we wait for dragons to flee.

The awakening sky
      beckons the blush of dawn
      subtle as a baby's breath,
      surprising as an unspoken love.

The wandering wind
      nudges the stars
      parts the clouds, clears a path
      for brilliant sun.

Slumberer wakes
        summoned by
        burnished rays
        that end the unlit hours.

November Gray

for Dolores

November's a gray month, a month to die in, a month to say goodbye in. Hospital efficiency and quiet corridors could not conceal the sound of harsh, labored breathing, the death rattle deep in her throat. The bleakness of November descended on the room. Dusk entered the window, settled over the bed, like angels' wings waiting to escort. Dim lighting conveyed an impending death, no brightness to reflect hope. A cheerless place to leave your best friend. A friendship that understood and accepted each other's frailties. A sister without the relationship.

Her face contorted with pain, surrounded by machines, threaded thru with plastic tubes: my dear friend was waiting. We knew, she and I that we would never again walk through fallen leaves, answer a telephone's ring, greet the familiar writing with delight. As she struggled to breathe I held her hand and whispered, "Go home, let go and go home." And she did. The shades of November changed from gray to black. My home was silent, the weariness I felt came from losing the struggle. We had both suffered. Words unspoken gave credence to our mutual trust in God. This was not the end.

When we meet again will our spirits be as young girls with dreams, young women with hopes, wives and mothers with sadness, or spirits that enfold all those stages of our lives. We will know each other, when November black turns to transforming light.

A Litany of Thanksgiving for the Sense of God in My World

Dawns of infinite grace   sunsets with flamboyant flair
     shadows laced with light   fields of yellow sunflowers
     birds on winds going nowhere   pine trees without ornaments
     a baby's smile as sweet as the love that bore her.

An inner Voice that comes as a sudden thought, a solution, or peace
     Laughter, blessings on all who hear it   a welcome telephone call
     Music, emotion from sadness to joy   garden bells rung by gentle winds
     A child's shout of pleasure   water lapping on shores
     thunder   Cardinal's spring song

A loving touch   soft, smooth skin of babies after their baths
     Rich black soil waiting to bloom   pansies made of velvet hues
     Warm bath, cool sheets   firm handshake
     wind slipping past   Spring's hesitant sunshine

Freshly cut grass   leaves burning in the fall   damp earth of March
        Clothes dried outdoors   flowers, most kinds   freshly baked bread
            Garlic and tomatoes   ocean's salty breeze   garden after rain
                    vanilla   lilacs and peonies

Sun ripened tomato off the vine   rutabagas   snow melting on the tongue
        Ice cream   lemonade   hot chocolate
            cool refreshing water   bread and butter

For all the goodness and sense of God I see in my world I give thanks.

For: My children, their spouses, and my grandchildren.
My nieces and nephews, who welcome me into their families.
My friends who know, love, and accept me.

Dreamfields

Its good to fall asleep here,
to sleep among the familiar.
Tomorrow is far away
past the dreamfields of the night.

We enter them each night,
(not always willingly)
that secluded space,
where the subconscious rules.

Shadowlike images whirl by
only to vanish beyond our grasp
and we, only visitors, are
unable to direct the scenes.

We battle the night terrors
here in known surroundings.
safe as we will ever be
before the dreamfields unfold.

To order additional copies of this book,
please send full amount plus $4.00 for
postage and handling for the first book and
50¢ for each additional book.

Send orders to:

Galde Press, Inc.
PO Box 460
Lakeville, Minnesota 55044-0460

Credit card orders call 1–800–777–3454
Phone (952) 891–5991 • Fax (952) 891–6091
Visit our website at http://www.galdepress.com

Write for our free catalog.